Good Friction, Bad Friction

Patty Whitehouse

Rourke
Publishing LLC
Vero Beach, Florida 32964

www.rourkepublishing.com

PHOTO CREDITS: © David and Patricia Armentrout: pages 4, 6, 7, 9, 14, 15, 19, 22; © Craig Lopetz: pages 5, 8, 12, 20; © PIR: pages 10, 13, 17; © constructionphotographs.com: page 11; © Michael Efford: page 18; © Chris Pollack: page 21

Editor: Robert Stengard-Olliges

Cover and interior design by Nicola Stratford

Library of Congress Cataloging-in-Publication Data

Whitehouse, Patricia, 1958-
 Good friction, bad friction / Patty Whitehouse.
   p. cm. -- (Construction forces)
 Includes index.
 ISBN-10: 1-60044-190-4 (hardcover)
 ISBN-13: 978-1-60044-190-5 (hardcover)
 ISBN 1-59515-551-1 (softcover)
 1. Tribology--Juvenile literature. 2. Friction--Juvenile literature. 3. Lubrication and lubricants--Juvenile literature. 4. Building sites--Juvenile literature. I. Title. II. Series: Whitehouse, Patricia, 1958- Construction forces.
 TJ1075.W45 2007
 531'.4--dc22
                            2006008859

Printed in the USA

CG/CG

Rourke Publishing

www.rourkepublishing.com – sales@rourkepublishing.com
Post Office Box 3328, Vero Beach, FL 32964
1-800-394-7055

Table of Contents

Construction Site

This is a **construction site**. People and **machines** work here.

Some things slip here. Some things stick. Sticking and slipping happen because of friction.

Things That Stick and Slide

Some things at a construction site slide or glide. Paint rollers glide on the walls.

Some things at a construction site stick or grip. Work gloves help to grip **tool** handles.

Friction

Friction is a **force**. It keeps the dirt from moving.

Some jobs need a lot of friction. Friction helps the
workers stay on the roof.

When Sliding is Good

A little friction holds the cable in place. It can slide up and down the crane.

The tank on the concrete mixer spins around. There is not much friction to stop the spinning.

When Sliding is Bad

The truck tire spins in the mud. It cannot grip. There is not enough friction.

This road has snow on it. Tires will slip. Snowy roads do not have much friction.

When Sticking is Good

Using tire chains gives tires more friction. Machines working in mud or snow need more friction.

The steps on the ladder are rough. Workers will not slip. This is a good place for friction.

When Sticking is Bad

Parts of this **engine** rub together. Friction might make the parts get too hot. Then the engine will not work.

The pipes on the scaffold are stuck. They rub together. There is too much friction.

Changing Friction

Adding **oil** makes less friction. People put oil into engines. Then the engine parts slide.

A truck adds sand to an icy road. The tire grips the sand. Now there is more friction.

Brakes and Friction

All trucks use brakes to stop. Brakes use friction to work.

Brake Pedal

Drivers step on the brake pedal. Stepping on the brakes adds friction.

Try It!

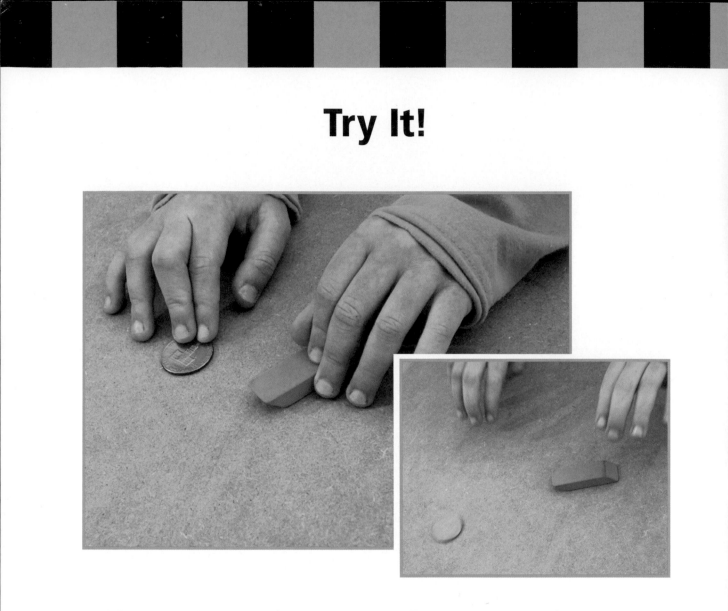

You can have a friction race. Put a coin and eraser on a slide. Let go to see what friction will do.

GLOSSARY

construction site (kuhn STRUHKT shun SITE): a place where workers build

engine (EN jun): part of a car or truck that makes it move

force (FORSS): a push or a pull

oil (OIL): liquid that makes things slippery

machine (muh SHEEN): something that uses energy to help people work

tool (TOOL): something used to do work

INDEX

FURTHER READING

Parker, Steve. *Forces and Motion.* Chelsea House Publishers, 2005.
Trumbauer, Lisa. *What is Friction?* Children's Press, New York: 2004.
Whyman, Kathryn. *Forces in Action.* Stargazer Books, 2005.

WEBSITES TO VISIT

http://www.bbc.co.uk/schools/revisewise/science/physical/12b_act.shtml
http://science.howstuffworks.com/engineering-channel.htm
http://www.bobthebuilder.com/usa/index.html

ABOUT THE AUTHOR

Patty Whitehouse has been a teacher for 17 years. She is currently a Lead Science teacher in Chicago, where she lives with her husband and two teenage children. She is the author of more than 100 books about science for children.